D1785745

LOW FAT GOURMET

Consultant Editor:
Valerie Ferguson

southwater

Contents

Introduction

Eating a healthy, low fat diet has never been easier for people who appreciate good food. Today you can enjoy gourmet ingredients and creative dishes while keeping your fat intake to a minimum. You can entertain healthily in style without forgoing fine flavours.

This book explains how to plan a low fat diet and introduces the wide range of fat substitutes now available, so that you do not have to go without rich or creamy dishes. The recipes show how to use these ingredients so skilfully that you will scarcely notice you are eating less fat. Nutritional Notes for each recipe list the fat and calorie content per portion (optional extras are not included in the analysis).

There are sophisticated soups and starters (fat content no more than 6 g per portion); fabulous fish and seafood, chicken and meat, and vegetarian main courses (no more than 16 g fat per portion); and irresistible desserts (no more than 8 g fat per portion). The recipes are drawn from cuisines around the world and make full use of exotic flavourings, herbs and spices to produce the tastiest dishes for the discerning palate. You will be surprised how good low fat food can taste!

Planning a Low Fat Diet

Fat is necessary in the diet in order to provide the fat-soluble vitamins A, D, E and K, plus "essential" fatty acids, that we need for health, but surveys show that we are eating too much – particularly saturated fat. Current nutritional advice suggests that we should limit our daily fat intake to no more than 33% of total calories. In real terms this means that for an average intake of 2,000 calories a day, 33% of energy would come from 660 calories or 73 g/2½ oz fat. The following paragraphs show that reducing dietary fat need not be difficult.

How To Cut Down

Use The Fat & Calorie Content of Food chart as a guide to avoiding high fat foods or simply using less of them. Watch out for hidden fats in foods. For example, we tend to think of cakes as sweet foods, but usually more calories come from their fat content than sugar.

Above: Bread is nourishing and low in fat.

The red meats – lamb, beef and pork – are the highest in fat, so try to eat chicken and turkey more often. Always choose lean cuts of meat and remove the skin and any visible fat from both meat and poultry before cooking. Avoid meat products such as sausages and pâtés. Fish, particularly white fish and shellfish, have a lower fat content than meat.

Fresh vegetables and fruit, with the odd exception such as avocados, are naturally low in fat (provided minimal amounts of fat are used to cook them) and vital to a healthy diet; aim to eat five portions a day. Grains such as rice and pasta, as well as pulses and lentils all have a low fat content. Nuts are high in fat and should be eaten in small amounts. Pastry (other than filo) has no place in a low fat diet.

In gourmet cooking you will probably still wish to use butter and cream occasionally, but try substituting half fat spread and crème fraîche. The section on Low Fat Ingredients & Substitutes should prove useful.

Cooking Methods

Grill, poach and steam foods whenever you can. If you do fry foods, use as little fat as possible. Make sauces and stews by first cooking the onions and garlic in a small quantity of stock.

Fat Facts

Fat is made up of three main types of fatty acids: saturated, mono-unsaturated and polyunsaturated.

Saturated fatty acids are believed to raise blood cholesterol levels and are thus considered to be unhealthy in excess; they are found mainly in foods of animal origin, such as fatty meat dairy foods (cream, full fat milk, cheese) and eggs.

Mono-unsaturated fatty acids are generally considered healthy in moderation; olives and olive oil used in the Mediterranean diet are relatively high in mono-unsaturated fatty acids.

Polyunsaturated fatty acids are thought to promote a healthy blood circulation. They also provide "essential fatty acids", which are essential components of all cell membranes. Polyunsaturates are found in vegetable and seed oils and margarines derived from them, oily fish and lean meat.

Labelling

Look at labels when choosing food. Ingredients are always listed in order of quantity, so watch out for those with fat near the top, as nutritional labels can be misleading.

Low fat: contains less than half the fat of the standard product. Remember

Above: Steaming fish is a healthy and flavoursome method of cooking. You can use a fish kettle, or a steamer fitment inside your saucepan. Inexpensive bamboo steamers are available from oriental stores.

that some foods are very high in fat, so even if a product such as low fat spread has half the fat content of margarine it still contains quite a lot of fat (about 40%).

Reduced fat: contains less than 75% of the fat to be found in the standard product.

Low cholesterol: no more than 0.005% of the total fat is cholesterol.

High in polyunsaturates/low in saturates: contains at least 35% fat of which at least 45% of the fatty acids are polyunsaturated and not more than 25% saturated.

The Fat & Calorie Content of Food

The chart shows the weight of fat and the energy content of 25 g/1 oz of many of the foods used in this book.

	Fat (g)	Energy
Cereal, baking & preserves		
Filo pastry	0.79	69 Kcals/288 kJ
Flour, white	0.32	85 Kcals/383 kJ
Flour, wholemeal	0.55	78 Kcals/330 kJ
Honey	0.0	72 Kcals/307 kJ
Oats, rolled	2.30	94 Kcals/397 kJ
Pasta, white, cooked	0.12	26 Kcals/108 kJ
Polenta	0.82	85 Kcals/357 kJ
Rice, white, cooked	0.1	31 Kcals/128 kJ
Soy sauce	0.0	11 Kcals/46 kJ
Sugar	0.07	23 Kcals/420 kJ
Teriyaki sauce	0.0	14 Kcals/59 kJ
Eggs & oils		
Egg, boiled (half an egg)	2.7	37 Kcals/153 kJ
Egg, white	0.0	9 Kcals/38 kJ
Egg, yolk	7.6	85 Kcals/351 kJ
Oil, olive	25.0	225 Kcals/924 kJ
Oil, sunflower	25.0	225 Kcals/924 kJ
Poultry & meat		
Beef, roast, topside, lean	1.1	39 Kcals/165 kJ
Chicken, roast, meat only	1.4	37 Kcals/155 kJ
Chicken, roast, meat & skin	3.5	54 Kcals/226 kJ
Veal	1.1	39Kcals/165 kJ
Fish		
Anchovy fillets, canned in oil, drained	5.0	70 Kcals/291 kJ
Clams	0.15	19 Kcals/81 kJ
Cod	0.2	20 Kcals/84 kJ
Haddock	0.15	20 Kcals/86 kJ
Monkfish	0.1	17 Kcals/69 kJ
Mussels	0.45	19 Kcals/78 kJ
Prawns, cooked, no shell	0.2	25 Kcals/105 kJ
Sea bass	0.6	25 Kcals/105 kJ
Squid	0.42	20 Kcals/86 kJ
Trout, grilled	1.4	34 Kcals/141 kJ
Tuna	1.1	34 Kcals/143 kJ
Vegetables		
Asparagus, boiled	0.15	6 Kcals/26 kJ
Aubergine, boiled	0.10	4 Kcals/16 kJ
Carrots	0.07	9 Kcals/35 kJ
Chick-peas, tinned	0.72	29 Kcals/ 122kJ
Courgettes, boiled	0.1	5 Kcals/20 kJ

	Fat (g)	Energy
Fennel	0.05	3 Kcals/13 kJ
Globe artichokes, boiled	0.05	12 Kcals/49 kJ
Leeks, boiled	0.2	5 Kcals/22 kJ
Mushrooms	0.1	3 Kcals/14 kJ
Olives	2.75	26 Kcals/108 kJ
Onions	0.05	6 Kcals/25 kJ
Peas, boiled	0.2	17 Kcals/73 kJ
Peppers	0.1	4 Kcals/16 kJ
Potatoes, new, boiled	0.1	19 Kcals/78 kJ
Spinach	0.20	6 Kcals/26 kJ
Tomatoes	0.1	4 Kcals/18 kJ
Fruit & nuts		
Apple	0.1	11 Kcals/45 kJ
Apricots	0.025	8 Kcals/33 kJ
Blackcurrants	0.001	7 Kcals/29 kJ
Figs, fresh	0.075	11 Kcals/45 kJ
Mango	0.05	14 Kcals/60 kJ
Orange	0.0	9 Kcals/39 kJ
Pear	0.02	10 Kcals/42 kJ
Strawberries	0.0	7 Kcals/28 kJ
Almonds	14.0	153 Kcals/633 kJ
Cashews, roasted	12.7	153 Kcals/633 kJ
Hazelnuts	15.9	163 Kcals/671 kJ
Pine nuts	17.1	172 Kcals/710 kJ
Sesame seeds	14.5	150 Kcals/618 kJ
Dairy produce		
Butter	20.4	184 Kcals/758 kJ
Cheese, cottage	1.0	25 Kcals/103 kJ
Cheese, Gruyère	8.3	102 Kcals/424 kJ
Cheese, Parmesan	8.0	113 Kcals/470 kJ
Cheese, ricotta	2.75	36 Kcals/150 kJ
Cream, double	12.0	112 Kcals/462 kJ
Cream, single	4.8	49 Kcals/204 kJ
Crème fraîche, half fat	3.8	42 Kcals/173 kJ
Greek yogurt	2.3	29 Kcals/119 kJ
Greek yogurt, reduced fat	1.2	20 Kcals/84 kJ
Low fat spread (40%)	10.1	98 Kcals/401 kJ
Margarine	20.4	185 Kcals/760 kJ
Milk, semi-skimmed	0.4	11 Kcals/49 kJ
Milk, skimmed	0.0	8 Kcals/35 kJ
Yogurt, plain, low fat	0.3	13 Kcals/54 kJ
Alcohol		
Wine, red	0	17 Kcals/71 kJ
Wine, white	0	17 Kcals/69 kJ

Low Fat Ingredients & Substitutes

There are now many lower fat versions of fats and cheeses available. They can be found in your local supermarket or health food store. Read the labels carefully to ensure that they are suitable if you intend to cook with them.

Left: Well-flavoured oils and low fat spreads are invaluable ingredients when preparing gourmet meals.

Oils

Olive oil: use extra virgin when a recipe requires a strong flavour. For a lighter flavour use ordinary olive oil.
Sunflower oil: rich in polyunsaturates.

Spreads

Low fat spreads are ideal for spreading on breads and tea breads, though they are not all suitable for cooking with.
Reduced fat butter: this contains about 40% fat.
Low fat spread, rich buttermilk blend: made with a high proportion of buttermilk, this is low in fat. Some are suitable for cooking with.
Sunflower light: contains 40% fat, plus emulsified water and milk solids.
Olive oil reduced fat spread: this spread has a better flavour than some other low fat spreads.
Very low fat spread: contains 20–30% fat and is not suitable for baking.

Milk & Cheeses

Milk, cream and yogurt: replace whole milk with skimmed or semi-skimmed milk. Low fat yogurt and fromage frais make excellent alternatives to cream, and can be combined with flavourings to make fillings or toppings for cakes and desserts. Yogurt strained in muslin will become as thick as crème fraîche.
Fromage frais: this is a soft cheese available in two grades: virtually fat free (0.4% fat), and creamy (7.9% fat).
Crème fraîche: half fat crème fraîche has a fat content of 15%.
Low fat cheeses: there are a lot of reduced fat cheeses now available. Generally, harder cheeses have a higher fat content than soft cheeses. Choose mature cheese as you need less of it to give a good flavour.
Cottage cheese: a low fat soft cheese which is also available in a half fat form.
Quark: made from fermented skimmed milk, this soft, white cheese is virtually free of fat.
Curd cheese: this is a low fat soft cheese made with either skimmed or semi-skimmed milk and can be used instead of cream cheese.
Half fat Cheddar: this contains about 14% fat.

Mediterranean Leek & Fish Soup with Tomatoes

This chunky soup makes a robust and wonderfully aromatic yet low fat meal in a bowl. Serve it with crisp-baked croûtes.

Serves 4

INGREDIENTS
15 ml/1 tbsp olive oil
2 large thick leeks, white and green parts
    separated, both thinly sliced
5 ml/1 tsp crushed coriander seeds
good pinch of dried red chilli flakes
300 g/11 oz small salad potatoes, thickly sliced
200 g/7 oz can Italian peeled, chopped
    plum tomatoes
600 ml/1 pint/2½ cups fish or vegetable stock
150 ml/¼ pint/⅔ cup fruity white wine
1 bay leaf
1 star anise
strip of pared orange rind
good pinch of saffron strands
450 g/1 lb white fish fillets, such as
    monkfish, sea bass, cod or haddock
450 g/1 lb small squid, cleaned
250 g/9 oz raw peeled prawns
30–45 ml/2–3 tbsp chopped fresh
    flat leaf parsley
salt and freshly ground black pepper

TO SERVE
1 short French loaf, sliced and toasted

1 Heat the oil in a heavy saucepan over a low heat, then add the green part of the leeks, the coriander seeds and chilli flakes. Cook, stirring occasionally, for 5 minutes.

2 Add the potatoes and tomatoes and pour in the stock and wine. Add the bay leaf, star anise, orange rind and saffron. Bring to the boil, reduce the heat and part-cover the pan. Simmer for about 15 minutes, or until the potatoes are tender. Taste and adjust the seasoning.

3 Cut the fish into chunks. Cut the squid sacs into rectangles and score a criss-cross pattern into them without cutting right through.

Nutritional Notes	
Energy	323 Kcals/1360 kJ
Total fat	6 g
Saturated fat	0.6 g
Cholesterol	314.3 mg

4 Add the fish chunks to the soup and cook gently for 4 minutes. Add the prawns and cook for 1 minute. Add the squid and the shredded white part of the leek and cook, stirring occasionally, for a further 2 minutes.

5 Serve sprinkled with parsley and accompanied by the French bread.

Wild Mushroom Soup

Dried porcini have an intense flavour that will delight mushroom lovers.

Serves 4

INGREDIENTS
25 g/1 oz/½ cup dried porcini mushrooms,
   soaked in warm water for 30 minutes
15 ml/1 tbsp olive oil
2 leeks, thinly sliced
2 shallots, roughly chopped
1 garlic clove, roughly chopped
225 g/8 oz/3¼ cups fresh wild mushrooms,
   roughly chopped
about 1.2 litres/2 pints/5 cups beef stock
2.5 ml/½ tsp dried thyme
30 ml/2 tbsp single cream
salt and freshly ground black pepper
fresh thyme sprigs, to garnish

1 Strain the porcini, reserving the liquid. Finely chop the porcini and set aside. Heat the oil in a large saucepan. Add the leeks, shallots and garlic and cook gently for about 5 minutes.

2 Add the fresh mushrooms and stir over a medium heat for a few minutes until they begin to soften. Pour in the stock and bring to the boil. Add the porcini, reserved soaking liquid, dried thyme and seasoning. Simmer gently for 30 minutes, stirring occasionally.

3 Process about three-quarters of the soup in a food processor or blender until smooth. Return to the soup remaining in the pan, stir in the cream and heat through gently. Adjust the seasoning. Serve in warmed bowls, garnished with fresh thyme.

Nutritional Notes	
Energy	66 Kcals/276 kJ
Total fat	4.7 g
Saturated fat	1.2 g
Cholesterol	3.32 mg

North African Spiced Soup

Serves 6

INGREDIENTS

1 large onion, chopped
1.2 litres/2 pints/5 cups vegetable stock
5 ml/1 tsp ground cinnamon
5 ml/1 tsp ground turmeric
15 ml/1 tbsp grated fresh root ginger
pinch of cayenne pepper
2 carrots, diced
2 celery sticks, diced
400 g/14 oz can chopped tomatoes
450 g/1 lb floury potatoes, diced
5 saffron strands
400 g/14 oz can chick-peas, drained
30 ml/2 tbsp chopped fresh coriander
15 ml/1 tbsp lemon juice
salt and freshly ground black pepper

1 Place the onion in a large saucepan with 300 ml/½ pint/1¼ cups of the vegetable stock. Simmer gently for about 10 minutes.

2 Meanwhile, mix together the ground cinnamon, turmeric, ginger, cayenne and 30 ml/2 tbsp of stock to form a paste. Stir into the onion mixture with the carrots, celery and remaining stock.

3 Bring to the boil, reduce the heat, cover and gently simmer for 5 minutes. Add the tomatoes and potatoes, and simmer for a further 20 minutes.

4 Add the saffron, chick-peas, coriander and lemon juice. Season to taste and serve piping hot in warmed bowls.

Nutritional Notes	
Energy	181 Kcals/763 kJ
Total fat	2.6 g
Saturated fat	0 g
Cholesterol	0 mg

Cheese & Spinach Puffs

Serves 6

INGREDIENTS
150 g/5 oz cooked chopped spinach
175 g/6 oz/¾ cup cottage cheese
5 ml/1 tsp freshly grated nutmeg
2 egg whites
30 ml/2 tbsp freshly grated Parmesan cheese
salt and freshly ground black pepper

1 Preheat the oven to 220°C/425°F/
Gas 7. Oil six ramekin dishes. Mix the
spinach and cottage cheese together,
then add the nutmeg and seasoning.

2 Whisk the egg whites in a separate
bowl until stiff enough to hold soft
peaks. Fold them evenly into the
spinach mixture, using a spatula or
large metal spoon, then spoon the
mixture into the ramekins, dividing it
evenly, and smooth the tops.

3 Sprinkle with the Parmesan and
place on a baking sheet. Bake for
15–20 minutes, or until well risen
and golden brown. Serve.

Nutritional Notes	
Energy	47 Kcals/195 kJ
Total fat	1.32 g
Saturated fat	0.52 g
Cholesterol	2.79 mg

Right: Cheese & Spinach Puffs (top);
Lemony Stuffed Courgettes

Lemony Stuffed Courgettes

Serves 4

INGREDIENTS
4 courgettes, about 175 g/6 oz each
5 ml/1 tsp sunflower oil
1 garlic clove, crushed
5 ml/1 tsp ground lemon grass
finely grated rind and juice of ½ lemon
115 g/4 oz/1½ cups cooked long grain rice
175 g/6 oz cherry tomatoes, halved
30 ml/2 tbsp toasted cashew nuts
salt and freshly ground black pepper
fresh thyme sprigs, to garnish

1 Preheat the oven to 200°C/400°F/
Gas 6. Halve the courgettes lengthways
and use a teaspoon to scoop out the
centres. Blanch the shells in boiling
water for 1 minute, then drain well.

2 Chop the courgette flesh and place
in a pan with the oil and garlic. Stir
until softened, but not browned.

3 Stir in the remaining ingredients and
spoon into the courgette shells. Place in
a baking tin and cover with foil. Bake
for 25–30 minutes, or until the shells
are tender. Serve garnished with thyme.

Nutritional Notes	
Energy	126 Kcals/530 kJ
Total fat	5.33 g
Saturated fat	0.65 g
Cholesterol	0 mg

Roasted Pepper Salad

Serves 4

INGREDIENTS
3 red peppers
6 large plum tomatoes
2.5 ml/½ tsp dried red chilli flakes
1 red onion, thinly sliced
3 garlic cloves, finely chopped
finely grated rind and juice of 1 lemon
45 ml/3 tbsp chopped fresh flat leaf parsley
20 ml/4 tsp extra virgin olive oil
salt and freshly ground black pepper
25 g/1 oz black and green olives and extra
    chopped fresh flat leaf parsley, to garnish

1 Preheat the oven to 220°C/425°F/
Gas 7. Place the peppers on a baking
sheet and roast, turning occasionally,
for 10 minutes or until the skins are
almost blackened. Add the tomatoes
and bake for 5 minutes.

2 Place the peppers in a plastic bag,
close the top loosely, trapping in the
steam, and leave until cool enough to
handle. Peel and deseed the peppers
and peel the tomatoes. Roughly chop
the peppers and tomatoes and place
them in a bowl.

3 Add the chilli flakes, onion, garlic,
lemon rind and juice and parsley. Mix
well, then transfer to a serving dish.
Season, drizzle over the oil and scatter
the olives and extra parsley over the top
to garnish. Serve at room temperature.

Nutritional Notes	
Energy	78 Kcals/323 kJ
Total fat	4.9 g
Saturated fat	0.8 g
Cholesterol	0 mg

Artichoke Salad

Serves 4

INGREDIENTS
6 small globe artichokes
juice of 1 lemon
15 ml/1 tbsp olive oil
2 onions, roughly chopped
175 g/6 oz/1 cup fresh or frozen broad beans
   (shelled weight), blanched and skinned
175 g/6 oz/1½ cups fresh or frozen peas
   (shelled weight)
120 ml/4 fl oz/½ cup white wine vinegar
15 ml/1 tbsp caster sugar
handful of fresh mint leaves, roughly torn
salt and freshly ground black pepper
fresh mint leaves, to garnish

1 Peel and discard the outer leaves from the artichokes and cut into quarters. Place the artichokes in a bowl of water with the lemon juice.

2 Heat the olive oil in a large pan and fry the onions until golden, stirring occasionally.

3 Drain the artichokes and add to the pan. Pour in 300 ml/½ pint/1¼ cups salted water, bring to the boil, then cook, covered, for 10 minutes.

4 Add the peas and broad beans and cook for 5 minutes, stirring occasionally until tender. Strain, and place all the vegetables in a bowl. Season with pepper. Leave to cool, then chill.

5 To make the salsa, gently heat the vinegar, sugar and mint in a saucepan until the sugar has dissolved. Simmer for 5 minutes, stirring occasionally. Remove from the heat and cool. To serve, drizzle the salsa over the vegetables and garnish with mint leaves.

Nutritional Notes	
Energy	182 Kcals/759 kJ
Total fat	4 g
Saturated fat	0.6 g
Cholesterol	5.5 mg

Fresh Tuna Shiitake Teriyaki

Teriyaki is a sweet soy marinade usually used to glaze meat, but here it enhances tuna steaks for a simple-to-prepare yet utterly delicious dish.

Serves 4

INGREDIENTS
4 x 175 g/6 oz fresh
   tuna steaks
salt
150 ml/¼ pint/⅔ cup teriyaki sauce
175 g/6 oz/2½ cups shiitake
   mushrooms, sliced
225 g/8 oz mooli
2 large carrots
boiled rice, to serve

2 Preheat a moderate grill or barbecue. Remove the tuna from the marinade and reserve the marinade. Cook the tuna steaks for 8 minutes, turning once.

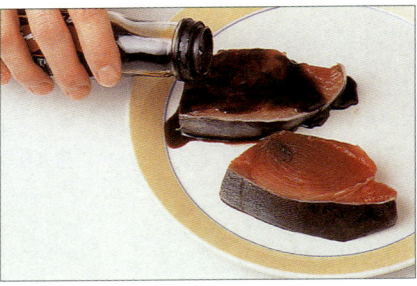

1 Season the tuna steaks with a light sprinkling of salt, then set aside for 20 minutes for it to penetrate the fish. Pour the teriyaki sauce over the tuna and marinate for a further 20–30 minutes, or for longer if you have sufficient time.

3 Transfer the teriyaki marinade to a stainless-steel saucepan and add the sliced shiitake mushrooms. Simmer for 3–4 minutes.

COOK'S TIP: One of the finest teriyaki sauces is made by Kikkoman and can be found in most large supermarkets.

Nutritional Notes	
Energy	286 Kcals/1188 kJ
Total fat	8.5 g
Saturated fat	2.7 g
Cholesterol	49 mg

4 Slice the mooli and carrot thinly, then shred finely with a chopping knife. Arrange in heaps on four serving plates and add the fish, with the mushrooms and sauce poured over. Serve with plain boiled rice.

Monkfish with Asparagus & Pears

With a flavour that is often likened to lobster meat, monkfish makes a superb gourmet meal which is low in fat.

Serves 4

INGREDIENTS
15 ml/1 tbsp sunflower oil
knob of butter, for flavouring (optional)
1 medium onion, sliced
1 garlic clove, crushed
2 courgettes, diagonally sliced
2 firm dessert pears, cored and sliced
675 g/1½ lb monkfish tail, skinned, boned and cut into chunks
175 ml/6 fl oz/¾ cup medium-dry white wine or cider
175 ml/6 fl oz/¾ cup fish stock
225 ml/8 oz asparagus spears, trimmed
strip of pared lemon rind
few fresh dill sprigs
45 ml/3 tbsp half fat crème fraîche
10 ml/2 tsp cornflour
salt and freshly ground black pepper

1 Heat the oil and butter, if using, in a large frying pan. Cook the onion, garlic, courgettes and pears over a gentle heat for about 5 minutes, or until the onion is just beginning to brown.

Nutritional Notes	
Energy	290 Kcals/1210 kJ
Total fat	10.5 g
Saturated fat	4 g
Cholesterol	55 mg

2 Using a slotted spoon, transfer the mixture to a plate. Add the monkfish chunks to the fat remaining in the pan and cook for 2–3 minutes, turning frequently, until lightly browned on both sides.

3 Pour in the white wine or cider and fish stock and return the vegetables and fruit to the pan. Add the asparagus spears and lemon rind. Season with salt and freshly ground black pepper. Bring to the boil, then lower the heat, cover the pan and simmer gently for about 8 minutes.

4 Add a few dill sprigs, reserving some for the garnish, and replace the lid. Simmer for 4–7 minutes more until both the fish and the asparagus are tender. Discard the dill and, using a slotted spoon, remove the fish, fruit and vegetables to a warmed serving dish and keep hot.

5 Mix the crème fraîche with the cornflour in a small bowl, then stir the mixture into the juices remaining in the pan. Cook over a gentle heat, stirring constantly, until thickened. Pour the sauce over the fish, garnish with the reserved dill and serve.

Chinese-style Steamed Fish

This is a classic Chinese way of cooking whole fish, with garlic, spring onions, ginger and black beans, but very little fat.

Serves 4

INGREDIENTS

2 sea bass, grey mullet or trout,
    about 675–800 g/1½–1¾ lb each
25 ml/1½ tbsp salted black beans
2.5 ml/½ tsp sugar
30 ml/2 tbsp finely shredded fresh
    root ginger
4 garlic cloves, thinly sliced
30 ml/2 tbsp Chinese rice wine or dry sherry
30 ml/2 tbsp light soy sauce
4–6 spring onions, finely shredded or
    sliced diagonally
15 ml/1 tbsp groundnut oil
10 ml/2 tsp sesame oil

3 Place a little shredded ginger and garlic slices inside the cavity of each fish and then lay them on a heatproof plate or dish that will fit inside your steamer. Rub the bean mixture into the fish, especially into the slashes, then scatter the remaining ginger and garlic over the top. Cover and chill for 30 minutes.

1 Wash the fish inside and out under cold running water, then pat dry with kitchen paper. Using a sharp knife, slash three or four deep cross shapes on each side of each fish.

2 Mash half the black beans with the sugar in a small bowl and then stir in the remaining whole beans.

4 Prepare a large steamer over a pan of boiling water. Sprinkle the rice wine or sherry and half the soy sauce over the fish and steam them for 15–20 minutes, or until just cooked.

5 Sprinkle with the remaining soy sauce and scatter the spring onions over the fish.

6 In a small saucepan, heat the groundnut oil until smoking, then trickle it over the spring onions. Sprinkle with the sesame oil and serve.

Nutritional Notes	
Energy	370 Kcals/1554 kJ
Total fat	12 g
Saturated fat	2.1 g
Cholesterol	240.2 mg

Grilled Snapper with Mango Salsa

This zingy fruit sauce is a wonderful way of making simply grilled fish into a special dish.

Serves 4

INGREDIENTS
350 g/12 oz new potatoes
3 eggs
115 g/4 oz green beans, topped, tailed
    and halved
4 red snapper, about 350 g/12 oz each,
    scaled and gutted
30 ml/2 tbsp olive oil
175 g/6 oz mixed lettuce leaves
10 cherry tomatoes
salt and freshly ground black pepper

FOR THE SALSA
45 ml/3 tbsp chopped fresh coriander
1 ripe mango, peeled, stoned and diced
½ red chilli, seeded and chopped
2.5 cm/1 in piece fresh root ginger,
    peeled and grated
juice of 2 limes
generous pinch of celery salt

1 Cook the potatoes in a large pan of boiling salted water for 15–20 minutes, or until just tender. Drain and set aside.

Nutritional Notes	
Energy	405 Kcals/1702 kJ
Total fat	15.59 g
Saturated fat	2.06 g
Cholesterol	163.62 mg

2 In a separate pan, boil the eggs in water for 10 minutes. Meanwhile, cook the beans for 6 minutes in boiling salted water. Remove the eggs from the pan, plunge into cold water to cool, then peel and cut into quarters. Drain the beans and set aside.

3 Preheat a moderate grill. Slash each snapper three times on either side, moisten with oil and grill for about 12 minutes, turning once.

4 To make the salsa, place the coriander in a food processor or blender. Add the mango, chilli, ginger, lime juice and celery salt and process until smooth.

COOK'S TIP: The fish is cooked through when the tip of a knife can gently lift the flesh away from the central bone.

5 Moisten the lettuce leaves with olive oil and divide them among four large plates. Arrange the snapper over the lettuce and season to taste.

6 Halve the potatoes and tomatoes and distribute them with the beans and quartered hard-boiled eggs over the salad. Serve with the salsa dressing.

Turbot in Parchment

Cooking in parcels is a delicious and ideal way to cook fish with the minimum of fat and maximum flavour.

Serves 4

INGREDIENTS
2 carrots, cut into thin julienne strips
2 courgettes, cut into thin
    julienne strips
2 leeks, cut into thin julienne strips
1 fennel bulb, cut into thin
    julienne strips
2 tomatoes, peeled, seeded
    and diced
30 ml/2 tbsp chopped fresh dill,
    tarragon or chervil
4 turbot fillets, about 200 g/7 oz each,
    cut in half
20 ml/4 tsp olive oil
60 ml/4 tbsp white wine or
    fish stock
salt and freshly ground
    black pepper

1 Preheat the oven to 190°C/375°F/ Gas 5. Cut four pieces of non-stick baking paper, about 45 cm/18 in long. Fold each piece in half and cut into a heart shape.

2 Open out the paper hearts. Arrange one quarter of each of the vegetables next to the fold of each heart. Sprinkle with salt and pepper and half the chopped herbs.

3 Arrange two pieces of turbot fillet over each bed of vegetables, overlapping the thin end of one piece and the thicker end of the other. Sprinkle the remaining herbs, the olive oil and wine or stock evenly over the fish.

4 Fold the top half of one of the paper hearts over the fish and vegetables and, beginning at the rounded end, fold the edges of the paper over, twisting and folding to form an airtight packet. Repeat with the remaining three.

COOK'S TIP: The parcels may be assembled up to 4 hours in advance and chilled.

5 Slide the parcels on to one or two baking sheets and bake for about 10 minutes, or until the paper is lightly browned and well puffed. Slide each parcel on to a warmed plate and serve immediately.

Nutritional Notes	
Energy	265 Kcals/1104 kJ
Total fat	9.2 g
Saturated fat	1.6 g
Cholesterol	0 mg

Trenette with Shellfish

Colourful and delicious, this pasta dish is perfect for a low fat supper.

Serves 6

INGREDIENTS
20 ml/4 tsp olive oil
1 small onion, finely chopped
1 garlic clove, crushed
½ red chilli, seeded and
    finely chopped
200 g/7 oz can chopped tomatoes
30 ml/2 tbsp chopped fresh
    flat leaf parsley
450 g/1 lb fresh clams in their
    shells, scrubbed
450 g/1 lb fresh mussels in their
    shells, scrubbed
60 ml/4 tbsp dry white wine
450 g/1 lb/4 cups dried trenette
a few fresh basil leaves
90 g/3½ oz/⅔ cup cooked peeled prawns,
    thawed and thoroughly dried
    if frozen
salt and freshly ground
    black pepper
chopped fresh herbs and lemon wedges,
    to garnish

1 Heat half the olive oil in a medium-sized frying pan. Add the chopped onion, crushed garlic and chilli and cook over a medium heat for 1–2 minutes, stirring continuously. Stir in the chopped tomatoes, half the fresh parsley and add pepper to taste. Bring to the boil, cover, reduce the heat and simmer for 15 minutes, stirring occasionally.

2 In a large saucepan, heat the remaining oil. Discard any clams or mussels that do not close when tapped sharply on a work surface, and add the rest to the pan. Add the remaining parsley and toss over a high heat for a few seconds. Pour in the white wine, cover tightly and cook for about 5 minutes, shaking the pan frequently, until the shellfish have opened.

3 Remove the pan from the heat and transfer the clams and mussels to a bowl using a slotted spoon, discarding any that have failed to open.

4 Strain the cooking liquid into a measuring jug and set aside. Reserve a few clams and mussels in their shells, then remove the rest from their shells.

Nutritional Notes	
Energy	414 Kcals/1755 kJ
Total fat	5 g
Saturated fat	0.7 g
Cholesterol	21 mg

5 Cook the pasta in a large saucepan of boiling salted water, according to the packet instructions, until *al dente*. Meanwhile, add 120 ml/4 fl oz/½ cup of the seafood liquid to the tomato sauce. Bring to the boil over a high heat, stirring. Reduce the heat, tear in the basil and add the prawns with the shelled clams and mussels. Stir well, then adjust the seasoning to taste.

6 Drain the pasta and tip it into a warmed bowl. Add the seafood sauce and toss well to combine. Serve sprinkled with chopped herbs and garnish each portion with the reserved clams and mussels and a lemon wedge.

Hunter's Chicken

This traditional Italian dish combines chicken in a flavourful tomato, mushroom and herb sauce to create a tempting low fat main course.

Serves 4

INGREDIENTS
15 g/½ oz/¼ cup dried porcini mushrooms
10 ml/2 tsp olive oil
4 small chicken portions on the bone, skinned
1 large onion, thinly sliced
400 g/14 oz can chopped tomatoes
150 ml/¼ pint/⅔ cup red wine
1 garlic clove, crushed
leaves of 1 sprig rosemary, finely chopped
115 g/4 oz/1¾ cups thinly sliced fresh
    field mushrooms
salt and freshly ground black pepper
fresh rosemary sprigs, to garnish
mashed potato or polenta, to serve (optional)

1 Put the porcini in a bowl, add 250 ml/8 fl oz/1 cup warm water and leave to soak for 20–30 minutes. Remove from the liquid and squeeze over the bowl. Strain the liquid and reserve. Finely chop the porcini.

2 Heat the oil in a large, flameproof casserole. Add the chicken and sauté over a medium heat for 5 minutes or until golden. Remove and drain on kitchen paper.

3 Add the sliced onion and chopped porcini mushrooms to the pan. Cook gently, stirring frequently, for about 3 minutes until the onion has softened but not browned.

4 Stir in the chopped tomatoes, wine and reserved mushroom soaking liquid, then add the crushed garlic and chopped rosemary, with salt and pepper to taste. Bring to the boil, stirring all the time.

5 Return the chicken to the pan and turn to coat it with the sauce. Cover and simmer gently for 30 minutes.

6 Add the fresh mushrooms and stir well to mix into the sauce. Continue simmering gently for 10 minutes or until the chicken is tender. Adjust the seasoning to taste. Serve hot, garnished with fresh rosemary sprigs, and accompanied by mashed potato or polenta, if you wish.

Nutritional Notes	
Energy	190 Kcals/801 kJ
Total fat	5 g
Saturated fat	1.3 g
Cholesterol	44.12 mg

Chicken with Lemon Sauce

Succulent chicken with a refreshing lemony sauce and just a hint of lime is a sure winner.

Serves 4

INGREDIENTS
4 small skinless, boneless chicken breasts
5 ml/1 tsp sesame oil
15 ml/1 tbsp dry sherry
1 egg white, lightly beaten
30 ml/2 tbsp cornflour
15 ml/1 tbsp vegetable oil
salt and freshly ground white pepper
chopped fresh coriander leaves and spring
    onions and lemon wedges, to garnish

FOR THE SAUCE
45 ml/3 tbsp fresh lemon juice
30 ml/2 tbsp lime cordial
45 ml/3 tbsp caster sugar
10 ml/2 tsp cornflour
90 ml/6 tbsp cold water

2 Mix together the egg white and cornflour. Add the mixture to the chicken and turn the chicken with tongs until thoroughly coated.

3 Heat the vegetable oil in a non-stick frying pan or wok and fry the chicken fillets for about 15 minutes, or until they are golden brown on both sides.

1 Arrange the chicken breasts in a single layer in a shallow bowl. Mix the sesame oil with the dry sherry and add 2.5 ml/½ tsp salt and 1.5 ml/¼ tsp pepper. Pour over the chicken, cover and marinate for 15 minutes.

4 Meanwhile, to make the sauce, combine all the ingredients in a small pan. Add 1.5 ml/¼ tsp salt. Bring to the boil over a low heat, stirring constantly, until the sugar has dissolved, and the sauce is smooth and has thickened slightly.

5 Cut the chicken into pieces and arrange on a warmed serving plate. Pour the lemon and lime sauce over, garnish with the coriander leaves, spring onions and lemon wedges, and serve immediately.

Nutritional Notes	
Energy	314 Kcals/1464 kJ
Total fat	6.5 g
Saturated fat	1.2 g
Cholesterol	117 mg

Chicken, Carrot & Leek Parcels

These intriguing parcels seal in all the juices and flavour. They are delicious on their own or served with new potatoes.

Serves 4

INGREDIENTS
2 small leeks, sliced
4 skinless, boneless chicken breasts
2 carrots, grated
2 pitted black olives, chopped
1 garlic clove, crushed
4 canned anchovy fillets, drained and
  halved lengthways
salt and freshly ground
  black pepper
black olives and fresh herb sprigs,
  to garnish

1 Preheat the oven to 200°C/400°F/ Gas 6. Cut out four sheets of lightly greased greaseproof paper, about 23 cm/9 in square.

2 Divide the sliced leeks equally among the paper squares. Put a piece of chicken on top of each pile of leeks and season well.

3 Mix the grated carrots, olives and garlic together. Season lightly and place on top of the chicken portions. Top each with two of the anchovy fillet halves.

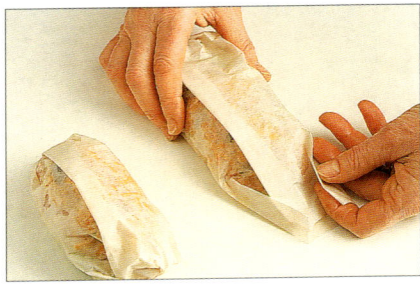

4 Carefully wrap up each parcel by bringing up the two sides of paper to the middle and folding them over into a tight double fold. Fold the corners in at each end and tuck underneath. Bake for 20 minutes or until the chicken is cooked. Serve hot, in the paper, garnished with black olives and herb sprigs.

Nutritional Notes	
Energy	154 Kcals/651 kJ
Total fat	2.37 g
Saturated fat	0.45 g
Cholesterol	78.75 mg

VARIATION: Skinless, boneless chicken is low in fat and is an excellent source of protein. Small, skinless turkey breast fillets also work well in this recipe and make a tasty change.

Veal with Tomatoes & White Wine

This famous Italian dish makes a hearty but low fat main course for special occasions. A green salad is the perfect accompaniment.

Serves 4

INGREDIENTS
30 ml/2 tbsp plain flour
4 pieces lean veal shank
2 small onions
10 ml/2 tsp olive oil
1 large celery stick, finely chopped
1 carrot, finely chopped
2 garlic cloves, finely chopped
400 g/14 oz can chopped tomatoes
300 ml/½ pint/1¼ cups dry
    white wine
300 ml/½ pint/1¼ cups chicken or
    veal stock
1 strip thinly pared lemon rind
2 bay leaves, plus extra
    for garnishing
salt and freshly ground
    black pepper

FOR THE GREMOLATA
30 ml/2 tbsp finely chopped fresh
    flat leaf parsley
finely grated rind of 1 lemon
1 garlic clove, finely chopped

1 Preheat the oven to 160°C/325°F/ Gas 3. Season the flour with salt and pepper and spread it out in a shallow bowl. Add the pieces of veal and turn them in the flour until they are evenly coated. Shake off any excess flour.

2 Slice one of the onions into rings. Heat the olive oil in a large, flameproof casserole, then add the veal pieces, with the onion rings, and brown the veal on both sides over a medium heat. Remove the veal with tongs, place on a plate and set aside to drain.

3 Chop the remaining onion and add to the pan with the celery, carrot and garlic. Stir the bottom of the pan to mix in the juices and sediment. Cook gently, stirring frequently, for about 5 minutes until the vegetables soften slightly.

4 Add the tomatoes, wine, stock, lemon rind and bay leaves, then season to taste. Bring to the boil, stirring.

5 Return the veal pieces to the pan and stir to coat thoroughly with the sauce. Cover and cook in the oven for 2 hours or until the veal feels tender when pierced with a fork.

6 Meanwhile, to make the gremolata, mix together the parsley, lemon rind and garlic in a small bowl. Remove the casserole from the oven and carefully discard the lemon rind and bay leaves. Adjust the seasoning to taste. Serve hot, sprinkled with the gremolata and garnished with bay leaves.

Nutritional Notes	
Energy	219 Kcals/919 kJ
Total fat	4.8 g
Saturated fat	1.2 g
Cholesterol	84.8 mg

Burgundy Steak & Mushroom Pie

Enjoy tender chunks of beef cooked in a rich wine sauce under a crisp filo pastry crust without piling on the calories.

Serves 4

INGREDIENTS

1 onion, finely chopped
175 ml/6 fl oz/¾ cup beef stock
450 g/1 lb lean chuck steak, cut into
    2.5 cm/1 in cubes
120 ml/4 fl oz/½ cup dry
    red wine
45 ml/3 tbsp plain flour
225 g/8 oz/3 cups chestnut
    mushrooms, halved
5 sheets filo pastry, thawed if frozen
45 ml/3 tbsp sunflower oil
salt and freshly ground
    black pepper
mashed potatoes and runner beans,
    to serve

1 Simmer the onion with 120 ml/
4 fl oz/½ cup of the stock in a large, covered, non-stick saucepan for
5 minutes. Uncover and continue to cook, stirring occasionally, until the stock has reduced entirely. Transfer to a plate and set aside until required.

2 Add the steak to the saucepan and dry-fry until the meat is lightly browned. Return the onions to the saucepan with the remaining stock and the red wine. Cover and simmer gently for about 1½ hours or until tender.

3 Preheat the oven to 190°C/375°F/ Gas 5. Blend the flour with 45 ml/
3 tbsp cold water, add to the saucepan and simmer, stirring all the time until the sauce has thickened.

4 Add the mushrooms and continue to cook for 3 minutes. Season to taste and spoon into a 1.2 litre/2 pint/
5 cup pie dish.

5 Brush each sheet of filo pastry with a little of the oil, then crumple it up loosely and place, oil-side up, over the pie filling.

6 Bake the pie in the oven for 25–30 minutes, or until the pastry is golden brown and crisp. Serve with mashed potatoes and crisp, steamed runner beans.

Nutritional Notes	
Energy	313 Kcals/1301 kJ
Total fat	9.1 g
Saturated fat	3.1 g
Cholesterol	70.9 mg

Provençale Stuffed Peppers

These colourful stuffed peppers are easy to make for a light and healthy lunch or supper without sacrificing flavour.

Serves 4

INGREDIENTS
10 ml/2 tsp olive oil
1 red onion, sliced
1 courgette, diced
115 g/4 oz/1¾ cups sliced mushrooms
1 garlic clove, crushed
400 g/14 oz can tomatoes
15 ml/1 tbsp tomato purée
25 g/1 oz/¼ cup pine nuts (optional)
30 ml/2 tbsp chopped fresh basil,
    plus whole leaves to garnish
2 large yellow peppers
2 large red peppers
25 g/1 oz/⅓ cup finely grated Parmesan or
    Fontina cheese (optional)
salt and freshly ground
    black pepper
chopped fresh herbs, to garnish

2 Stir in the tomatoes and tomato purée, then bring to the boil and simmer, uncovered, for 10–15 minutes, stirring occasionally, until thickened slightly. Remove the pan from the heat and stir in the pine nuts, if using, the chopped basil and seasoning. Set aside.

3 Cut the peppers in half lengthways and remove the seeds. Blanch the pepper halves in a saucepan of boiling water for about 3 minutes. Drain.

1 Preheat the oven to 180°C/350°F/ Gas 4. Heat the oil in a saucepan, add the onion, courgette, mushrooms and garlic and cook gently for 3 minutes, stirring occasionally.

4 Place the pepper halves cut-side up, in a shallow ovenproof dish and fill with the vegetable mixture. Cover the dish with foil.

5 Bake in the oven for 20 minutes. Uncover, sprinkle each pepper half with a little grated cheese, if using, and bake, uncovered, for a further 5–10 minutes. Serve garnished with chopped herbs and whole basil leaves.

Nutritional Notes	
Energy	70 Kcals/293 kJ
Total fat	2.5 g
Saturated fat	0.4 g
Cholesterol	0 mg

Red Pepper & Watercress Filo Parcels

Peppery watercress combines well with sweet red pepper in these crisp little pastries, which make a delightful lunch served with salad.

Serves 4

INGREDIENTS
3 red peppers
175 g/6 oz watercress
225 g/8 oz/1 cup ricotta cheese
50 g/2 oz/⅓ cup blanched almonds, toasted
   and chopped
8 sheets filo pastry, thawed if frozen
30 ml/2 tbsp olive oil
salt and freshly ground black pepper
salad leaves, to serve

1 Preheat the oven to 190°C/375°F/ Gas 5. Place the peppers under a hot grill until blistered and charred. Place in a plastic bag. When cool enough to handle, peel, seed and pat dry on kitchen paper.

2 Place the peppers and watercress in a food processor and pulse until coarsely chopped. Spoon into a bowl. Mix in the ricotta and almonds and season.

3 Working with one sheet of filo pastry at a time, cut out two 18 cm/ 7 in and two 5 cm/2 in squares from each sheet. Brush one large square with a little olive oil and place a second large square at an angle of 45 degrees to form a star shape. Keep the unused filo covered with a damp dish towel while preparing each parcel. This will stop the filo drying out.

4 Place one of the small squares in the centre of the star shape, brush lightly with olive oil and top with a second small square.

Nutritional Notes	
Energy	217 Kcals/904 kJ
Total fat	10.8 g
Saturated fat	2.8 g
Cholesterol	14.1 mg

5 Top with one-eighth of the red pepper mixture. Bring the edges together to form a purse shape and twist to seal. Place on a lightly greased baking sheet and bake the parcels for 25–30 minutes until golden. Serve with salad leaves.

Milanese Risotto

This traditional risotto is deliciously flavoured with garlic, shavings of Parmesan and fresh parsley to create a filling and tasty, low fat dish.

Serves 4

INGREDIENTS
5 ml/1 tsp (or 1 sachet) saffron strands
15 g/½ oz/1 tbsp butter
1 large onion, finely chopped
275 g/10 oz/1½ cups arborio rice
150 ml/¼ pint/⅔ cup dry
    white wine
1 litre/1¾ pints/4 cups hot
    vegetable stock
salt and freshly ground
    black pepper
15 g/½ oz shaved fresh Parmesan cheese,
    to serve

FOR THE GREMOLATA
2 garlic cloves, crushed
60 ml/4 tbsp chopped
    fresh parsley
finely grated rind of 1 lemon

1 To make the gremolata, mix together the garlic, parsley and lemon rind in a bowl. Cover with clear film and set aside.

2 Put the saffron in a small bowl with 15 ml/1 tbsp boiling water and leave to infuse. Melt the butter in a heavy-based saucepan and gently fry the onion for 5 minutes until softened and golden, stirring occasionally.

3 Stir in the rice and cook for about 2 minutes until it becomes translucent. Add the wine and saffron infusion and cook, stirring, for several minutes until all the liquid is absorbed.

4 Add 300 ml/½ pint/1¼ cups of the hot stock and simmer gently until it has been absorbed, stirring frequently.

5 Gradually add more stock, a ladleful at a time, until the rice is tender, stirring frequently. (The rice might be tender and creamy before you have added all the stock, so add it slowly towards the end.)

6 Season the risotto, remove from the heat, cover, and allow to stand for a minute. Serve, scattered with shavings of Parmesan and the gremolata.

Nutritional Notes	
Energy	258 Kcals/1090 kJ
Total fat	5 g
Saturated fat	2.6 g
Cholesterol	9.9 mg

Baked Cheese Polenta with Tomato Sauce

For this Italian-style dish, polenta is cooked in a similar way to porridge, allowed to set, then cut into shapes and baked. If possible, start preparations the day before so that the polenta can chill overnight.

Serves 6

INGREDIENTS
250 g/9 oz/2¼ cups quick-
    cook polenta
5 ml/1 tsp paprika
2.5 ml/½ tsp freshly grated nutmeg
5 ml/1 tsp olive oil
1 large onion, finely chopped
2 garlic cloves, crushed
2 x 400 g/14 oz cans
    chopped tomatoes
15 ml/1 tbsp tomato purée
5 ml/1 tsp sugar
50 g/2 oz/½ cup grated Gruyère
salt and freshly ground
    black pepper

1 Line a 28 x 18 cm/11 x 7 in baking tin with clear film. Bring 1 litre/1¾ pints/4 cups water to the boil in a large saucepan with 5 ml/ 1 tsp salt.

2 Pour in the polenta in a steady stream and cook for 5 minutes, stirring continuously. Beat in the paprika and nutmeg, then pour the mixture into the prepared tin and smooth the surface. Leave to cool, then chill for at least 1 hour or overnight, if possible.

3 Heat the oil in a non-stick saucepan and cook the onion and garlic until soft, stirring occasionally. Stir in the tomatoes, tomato purée, sugar and seasoning. Bring to the boil, reduce the heat and simmer for 20 minutes, stirring occasionally.

4 Preheat the oven to 200°C/400°F/ Gas 6. Turn the cooled polenta out on to a chopping board and cut evenly into 5 cm/2 in squares.

5 Place half the polenta squares in a greased ovenproof dish. Spoon over half the tomato sauce and sprinkle half the cheese over the top. Repeat the layers. Bake in the oven for about 25 minutes, or until golden. Serve hot.

Nutritional Notes	
Energy	223 Kcals/929 kJ
Total fat	5.1 g
Saturated fat	2.1 g
Cholesterol	8.3 mg

COOK'S TIP: Polenta squares can be grilled and served with the sauce. You could add some broad beans to the sauce and omit the cheese, if you like.

Potato Gratin

A simple but delicious way of oven-cooking potatoes as an accompaniment.

Serves 4

INGREDIENTS
1 garlic clove
5 large baking potatoes, peeled
45 ml/3 tbsp grated Parmesan cheese
600 ml/1 pint/2½ cups vegetable or
   chicken stock
pinch of freshly grated nutmeg
salt and freshly ground
   black pepper

1 Preheat the oven to 200°C/400°F/
Gas 6. Halve the garlic clove and rub
over the base and sides of a gratin dish
measuring about 20 x 30 cm/8 x 12 in.

VARIATION: For a potato and
onion gratin, thinly slice one medium
onion and layer with the potato.

2 Slice the potatoes very thinly and
arrange one-third of them in the dish.
Sprinkle with a little grated cheese, salt
and freshly ground black pepper. Pour
over some of the stock to prevent the
potatoes from discolouring.

3 Continue layering the potatoes and
cheese as before, then pour over the rest
of the stock. Sprinkle with the nutmeg.

4 Bake in the oven for 1¼–1½ hours,
or until the potatoes are tender and
the top layer well browned. Serve hot.

Nutritional Notes	
Energy	224 Kcals/931 kJ
Total fat	2.8 g
Saturated fat	1.4 g
Cholesterol	6.3 mg

Roasted Vegetables

Roasting vegetables with a little olive oil really intensifies their flavour.

Serves 4

INGREDIENTS
1 each red and yellow pepper, seeded and cut
    into large chunks
2 Spanish onions, cut into thick wedges
2 large courgettes, cut into large chunks
1 large aubergine, cut into
    large chunks
1 fennel bulb, thickly sliced
2 marmande or beef tomatoes, halved
8 fat garlic cloves, unpeeled
30 ml/2 tbsp olive oil
fresh rosemary sprigs
freshly ground black pepper

1 Preheat the oven to 220°C/425°F/
Gas 7. Spread the peppers, onions,
courgettes, aubergine, fennel and
tomatoes in a lightly oiled, shallow
ovenproof dish or roasting tin.

2 Tuck the unpeeled garlic cloves
among the vegetables chunks, then
brush them with the olive oil. Place
some fresh rosemary sprigs among the
vegetables and sprinkle over some
freshly ground black pepper, particularly on the tomatoes.

3 Roast for 20–25 minutes, carefully
turning the vegetables halfway through
the cooking time so that they brown
evenly. Serve the roasted vegetables
from the dish or tin or transfer to a flat
serving platter.

Nutritional Notes	
Energy	180 Kcals/755 kJ
Total fat	8 g
Saturated fat	1 g
Cholesterol	0 mg

Green Beans with Tomatoes

Gently simmered green beans with tomatoes, olives and dry white wine.

Serves 4

INGREDIENTS

15 ml/1 tbsp olive oil
1 large onion, finely sliced
2 garlic cloves, finely chopped
450 g/1 lb French green beans
6 large ripe plum tomatoes, peeled, seeded
    and coarsely chopped
150 ml/¼ pint/⅔ cup dry white wine
16 pitted black olives
10 ml/2 tsp lemon juice
salt and freshly ground black pepper

1 Heat the oil in a large frying pan. Add the onion and garlic and cook for 5 minutes, or until the onion is softened, stirring occasionally.

2 Halve the French beans lengthways. Add the tomatoes, wine, beans, olives and lemon juice to the onions, and cook over a gentle heat for a further 20 minutes, stirring occasionally, until the sauce is thickened and the beans are tender.

3 Season with salt and pepper to taste and transfer to a warmed serving dish. Serve at once.

Nutritional Notes	
Energy	69 Kcals/278 kJ
Total fat	2.7 g
Saturated fat	0.4 g
Cholesterol	0 mg

Orange Candied Sweet Potatoes

This truly scrumptious side dish could scarcely be lower in fat.

Serves 8

INGREDIENTS
900 g/2 lb sweet potatoes
250 ml/8 fl oz/1 cup orange juice
50 ml/2 fl oz/¼ cup maple syrup
5 ml/1 tsp grated fresh
   root ginger
7.5 ml/1½ tsp ground cinnamon, plus extra
   to garnish
6.5 ml/1¼ tsp ground cardamom
7.5 ml/1½ tsp salt
freshly ground black pepper
orange segments, to serve

1 Preheat the oven to 180°C/350°F/Gas 4. Peel and dice the potatoes and then boil in water for 5 minutes.

2 Meanwhile, in a bowl, stir the remaining ingredients together. Spread over the base of a shallow non-stick baking tin.

3 Drain the potatoes, place in the tin and stir well. Cook in the oven for 1 hour, stirring every 15 minutes, until the potatoes are tender and well coated. Sprinkle with ground cinnamon and serve with the orange segments.

Nutritional Notes	
Energy	117 Kcals/490 kJ
Total fat	0.4 g
Saturated fat	0.1 g
Cholesterol	0 mg

Poached Pears in Port Syrup

This beautiful dessert is the perfect choice for autumn entertaining.

Serves 4

INGREDIENTS
2 ripe, firm pears
thinly pared rind of 1 lemon
175 ml/6 fl oz/¾ cup ruby port
50 g/2 oz/¼ cup caster sugar
1 cinnamon stick
60 ml/4 tbsp cold water
half fat crème fraîche, to serve (optional)
15 ml/1 tbsp sliced hazelnuts, toasted and
    fresh mint leaves, to decorate

1 Peel the pears, halve them and remove the cores. Place the lemon rind, port, sugar, cinnamon stick and water in a pan. Bring to the boil over a low heat. Add the pears, lower the heat, cover and poach for 5 minutes. Leave to cool.

2 When the pears are cold, transfer them to a bowl using a slotted spoon.

3 Return the sauce to the heat. Boil rapidly until it has reduced to form a syrup. Discard the cinnamon and lemon rind and leave the syrup to cool.

4 To serve, place each pear half in turn on a board, cut-side down. Keeping it intact at the stalk end, slice it lengthways, then, using a palette knife, carefully lift it off and place on a dessert plate. Press gently so that the pear fans out. Spoon over the port syrup. Top each portion with a few hazelnuts and mint leaves. Serve, with crème fraîche, if you like.

Nutritional Notes	
Energy	173 Kcals/725 kJ
Total fat	2.5 g
Saturated fat	0.17 g
Cholesterol	0 mg

Nectarine Meringues

Sheer indulgence – yet these tempting treats are low in fat.

Serves 5

INGREDIENTS
3 egg whites
175 g/6 oz/scant 1 cup caster sugar
50 g/2 oz/½ cup chopped
   hazelnuts, toasted
300 ml/½ pint/1¼ cups low fat
   Greek yogurt
15 ml/1 tbsp sweet dessert wine
2 nectarines, stoned and sliced
fresh mint sprigs, to decorate

1 Preheat the oven to 140°C/275°F/
Gas 1. Line two large baking sheets
with non-stick baking paper. Whisk
the egg whites in a grease-free bowl
until they form stiff peaks. Gradually
whisk in the sugar, a spoonful at a
time, until the mixture is glossy. Fold
in two-thirds of the hazelnuts.

2 Spoon ten ovals on to each baking
sheet. Scatter the remaining hazelnuts
over five of them. Flatten the other five.

3 Bake the meringues for 1–1¼ hours,
or until crisp and dry, then cool
completely on a wire rack.

4 Mix the yogurt with the wine.
Spoon some of this mixture on to each
of the plain meringues and top with
nectarine slices. Put each meringue on
a dessert plate with a hazelnut-topped
meringue. Serve decorated with mint.

Nutritional Notes	
Energy	293 Kcals/1236 kJ
Total fat	4.9 g
Saturated fat	2.34 g
Cholesterol	4.2 mg

Spiced Mango Filo Fingers

Mangoes have a wonderful texture and look great simply sliced and fanned out next to these low fat crunchy filo fingers.

Serves 8

INGREDIENTS
5 mangoes
6 sheets filo pastry, thawed if frozen
40 g/1½ oz/3 tbsp butter, melted
40 g/1½ oz/3 tbsp soft light
  brown sugar
20 ml/4 tsp ground cinnamon
icing sugar, for dusting

2 Keeping the rest of the filo covered with a damp dish towel, lay one sheet on a baking sheet and brush with melted butter. Mix the brown sugar and cinnamon together and sprinkle one-fifth of the mixture over the filo. Lay another sheet of filo on top and repeat the layers for the other four sheets, ending with a filo sheet.

1 Preheat the oven to 200°C/400°F/Gas 6. Set the two most perfect mangoes aside for the decoration. Peel the remaining mangoes and slice the flesh, discarding the stone. Cut the flesh across into 3 mm/⅛ in thick slices.

Nutritional Notes	
Energy	230 Kcals/958 kJ
Total fat	5.8 g
Saturated fat	3.1 g
Cholesterol	12.9 mg

3 Brush the top filo sheet with butter, trim off the excess pastry and lay the sliced mangoes in neat rows across the layered filo, to cover it completely. Brush with the remaining butter and bake for 30 minutes. Allow to cool on the baking sheet, then cut into eight fingers.

4 Slice the flesh from either side of the stone of the reserved mangoes. Cut each piece in half lengthways. Make four long cuts, almost to the end, in each quarter.

5 Dust the mango with icing sugar. Put on a plate and fan out the slices. Serve with the mango filo fingers.

55

Apple & Blackcurrant Pancakes

These pancakes are made with a wholewheat batter and are served with a delicious fruit mixture and, if you wish, half fat crème fraîche.

Serves 4

INGREDIENTS
115 g/4 oz/1 cup plain wholemeal flour
300 ml/½ pint/1¼ cups skimmed milk
1 egg, beaten
15 ml/1 tbsp sunflower oil, plus extra
    for greasing
half fat crème fraîche,
    to serve (optional)
toasted nuts or sesame seeds,
    for sprinkling (optional)

FOR THE FILLING
450 g/1 lb cooking apples
225 g/8 oz/2 cups blackcurrants
30–45 ml/2–3 tbsp water
30 ml/2 tbsp demerara sugar

2 To make the filling, quarter, peel and core the apples. Slice them into a pan and add the blackcurrants and water. Cook for 10–15 minutes over a gentle heat until the fruit is soft. Stir in enough demerara sugar to sweeten.

1 Place the flour in a mixing bowl and make a well in the centre. Add a little of the milk with the egg and the oil. Whisk the flour into the liquid, then gradually whisk in the rest of the milk, keeping the batter smooth and free from lumps. Cover and chill.

3 Lightly grease a pancake pan with just a smear of oil. Heat the pan, pour in about 30 ml/2 tbsp batter, swirl it around and cook for about 1 minute.

4 Flip the pancake over with a palette knife and cook the other side. Transfer to a plate and keep warm while cooking the remaining pancakes (unless cooking to order).

5 Fold the pancakes on individual serving plates. Top with some of the apple and blackcurrant mixture. Serve with a dollop of crème fraîche, if using, and sprinkle with nuts or sesame seeds, if liked.

Nutritional Notes	
Energy	120 Kcals/505 kJ
Total fat	3 g
Saturated fat	0.5 g
Cholesterol	25 mg

Apricot Parcels

An unusual filling of mincemeat, marzipan and ratafias is contained within an apricot and wrapped in a crisp filo purse.

Makes 8

INGREDIENTS
350 g/12 oz filo pastry, thawed if frozen
30 ml/2 tbsp low fat spread, melted
8 apricots, halved and stoned
60 ml/4 tbsp luxury mincemeat
12 ratafias, crushed
30 ml/2 tbsp grated marzipan
icing sugar, for dusting

1 Preheat the oven to 200°C/400°F/ Gas 6. Cut the filo into 32 squares each measuring 18 x 18 cm/7 x 7 in. Brush four of the squares with melted spread and stack them, giving each layer a quarter turn so that the stack acquires a star shape. Repeat to make eight stars.

2 Place the apricot halves, hollow up, on a chopping board. Mix together the mincemeat, crushed ratafias and grated marzipan and spoon a little of the mixture into the hollow in eight of the apricot halves.

3 Top each with an apricot half, then place one whole apricot in the centre of each pastry star. Bring the corners of the pastry together and squeeze to make a closed parcel in the shape of a purse.

4 Place the parcels on a baking sheet and brush each with a little melted spread. Bake for 15–20 minutes or until the pastry is golden and crisp. Lightly dust with icing sugar and serve immediately.

Nutritional Notes	
Energy	234 Kcals/982 kJ
Total fat	4.4 g
Saturated fat	1.1 g
Cholesterol	3.7 mg

COOK'S TIP: If you have run out of mincemeat, use dried mixed vine fruits mixed with a little pear and apple spread instead.

Creamy Mango Cheesecake

Proof that a truly delicious, low fat cheesecake does exist!

Serves 6

INGREDIENTS
115 g/4 oz/1 cup rolled oats
40 g/1½ oz/3 tbsp sunflower margarine
30 ml/2 tbsp clear honey
1 large ripe mango
300 g/10 oz/1¼ cups low fat soft cheese
150 g/5 oz/⅔ cup low fat plain yogurt
finely grated rind of 1 small lime
45 ml/3 tbsp apple juice
20 ml/4 tsp powdered gelatine
fresh mango and lime slices, to decorate

1 Preheat the oven to 200°C/400°F/Gas 6. Mix together the rolled oats, margarine and honey. Press the mixture into the base of a 20 cm/8 in loose-based cake tin. Bake for 12–15 minutes until lightly browned. Cool.

2 Peel, stone and roughly chop the mango. Place the chopped mango, cheese, yogurt and lime rind in a food processor and process until smooth.

3 Heat the apple juice until boiling, sprinkle the gelatine over it, stirring to dissolve. Stir into the cheese mixture.

4 Pour the cheese mixture into the tin and chill until set, then turn out on to a serving plate. Decorate the top with mango and lime slices before serving.

Nutritional Notes	
Energy	281 Kcals/1183 kJ
Total fat	7.58 g
Saturated fat	1.47 g
Cholesterol	1.97 mg

Fresh Figs with Honey & Wine

Naturally sweet fresh figs taste wonderful in a honeyed wine syrup.

Serves 6

INGREDIENTS
450 ml/¾ pint/scant 2 cups dry white wine
75 g/3 oz/⅓ cup clear honey
50 g/2 oz/¼ cup caster sugar
1 small orange
8 cloves
450 g/1 lb fresh figs
1 cinnamon stick
bay leaves, to decorate

FOR THE SAUCE
300 ml/½ pint/1¼ cups low fat Greek yogurt
5 ml/1 tsp pure vanilla essence
5 ml/1 tsp caster sugar

1 Put the wine, honey and sugar in a heavy-based saucepan and heat gently until the sugar dissolves.

2 Stud the orange with the cloves and add to the syrup with the figs and cinnamon. Cover and simmer for 10 minutes, or until the figs are soft. Transfer to a serving dish and cool.

3 To make the sauce, flavour the yogurt with the vanilla essence and sugar. Spoon it into a serving bowl. Cut one or two of the figs in half, if you like, to show off their pretty centres. Decorate with the bay leaves and serve with the yogurt sauce.

Nutritional Notes	
Energy	201 Kcals/845 kJ
Total fat	2.7 g
Saturated fat	1.58 g
Cholesterol	3.5 mg

Strawberry & Lavender Sorbet

Serves 6

INGREDIENTS
150 g/5 oz/¾ cup caster sugar
300 ml/½ pint/1¼ cups water
6 fresh lavender flowers, plus extra
   to decorate
500 g/1¼ lb/4 cups strawberries, hulled
1 egg white

1 Put the sugar and water into a saucepan and bring to the boil, stirring until the sugar has dissolved. Remove from the heat, add the lavender flowers and leave to infuse for 1 hour. Chill.

2 Purée the strawberries in a food processor, then press the purée through a large sieve into a bowl. Pour into an ice-cream maker and strain in the lavender syrup.

3 Churn for 20 minutes until thick. Alternatively, use a freezerproof container and freeze for 4 hours until mushy.

4 Whisk the egg white until just frothy. Add it to the ice-cream maker and continue to churn until the sorbet is firm enough to scoop. Alternatively, transfer the sorbet to a food processor, process until smooth, then add the egg white. Return the sorbet to the container and freeze for 4 hours, or until firm. Serve decorated with lavender.

Nutritional Notes	
Energy	125 Kcals/518 kJ
Total fat	0.1 g
Saturated fat	0 g
Cholesterol	0 mg

Iced Melon with Pimm's

Serves 6

INGREDIENTS

50 g/2 oz/¼ cup caster sugar
30 ml/2 tbsp clear honey
15 ml/1 tbsp lemon juice
60 ml/4 tbsp water
1 medium cantaloupe or Charentais melon,
    about 1 kg/2¼ lb
crushed ice, cucumber slices and borage
    leaves, to decorate
Pimm's No. 1, to serve

1 Put the sugar, honey, lemon juice and water in a small saucepan and heat gently until the sugar dissolves. Bring to the boil and boil for 1 minute.

2 Halve the melon and discard the seeds. Scoop the flesh into a food processor or blender, taking care to keep the half shells intact. Blend the flesh until smooth.

3 Scrape into a bowl, stir in the syrup and chill. Drain the shells on kitchen paper, then transfer to the freezer.

4 Churn the melon mixture in an ice-cream maker until it holds its shape. Alternatively, use a freezerproof container and freeze for 4 hours, then whisk until smooth. Pack it into the melon halves. Level the surface, then hollow out the centre. Freeze until firm.

5 Cut each melon half into three wedges. Place on a bed of crushed ice and decorate with cucumber and borage. Drizzle with Pimm's and serve.

Nutritional Notes	
Energy	72 Kcals/299 kJ
Total fat	0.2 g
Saturated fat	0 g
Cholesterol	0 mg

This edition is published by Southwater

Southwater is an imprint of
Anness Publishing Ltd
Hermes House
88–89 Blackfriars Road
London SE1 8HA
tel. 020 7401 2077
fax 020 7633 9499

Distributed in the USA by
Anness Publishing Inc.
27 West 20th Street
Suite 504, New York NY 10011

Distributed in the UK by
The Manning Partnership
251–253 London Road East
Batheaston
Bath BA1 7RL
tel. 01225 852 727
fax 01225 852 852

Distributed in Australia by
Sandstone Publishing
Unit 1, 360 Norton Street, Leichhardt
New South Wales 2040
tel. 02 9560 7888
fax 02 9560 7488

All rights reserved. No part of this publication may be reproduced, stored in a retrieval system, or transmitted in any way or by any means, electronic, mechanical, photocopying, recording or otherwise, without the prior written permission of the copyright holder.

© 2000 Anness Publishing Limited

1 3 5 7 9 10 8 6 4 2

Publisher: Joanna Lorenz
Editor: Valerie Ferguson
Series Designer: Bobbie Colgate Stone
Designer: Andrew Heath
Production Controller: Joanna King

Recipes contributed by: Catherine Atkinson,
Angela Boggiano, Jacqueline Clark,
Carole Clements, Joanna Farrow,
Christine France, Brian Glover, Sara Lewis,
Kathy Man, Sally Mansfield, Maggie Mayhew,
Annie Nichols, Maggie Pannell, Anne Sheasby,
Steven Wheeler, Elizabeth Wolf-Cohen,
Jeni Wright
Photography: Karl Adamson, James Duncan,
Gus Filgate, Michelle Garrett, Amanda Heywood,
Janine Hosegood, William Lingwood, Steve Moss,
Craig Robertson, Sam Stowell

Notes:
For all recipes, quantities are given in both metric
and imperial measures and, where appropriate,
measures are also given in standard cups
and spoons.
Follow one set, but not a mixture, because they
are not interchangeable.

Standard spoon and cup measures are level.

1 tsp = 5 ml   1 tbsp = 15 ml

1 cup = 250 ml/8 fl oz

Australian standard tablespoons are 20 ml.
Australian readers should use 3 tsp in place of
1 tbsp for measuring small quantities of gelatine,
cornflour, salt etc.

Medium eggs are used unless otherwise stated.

64

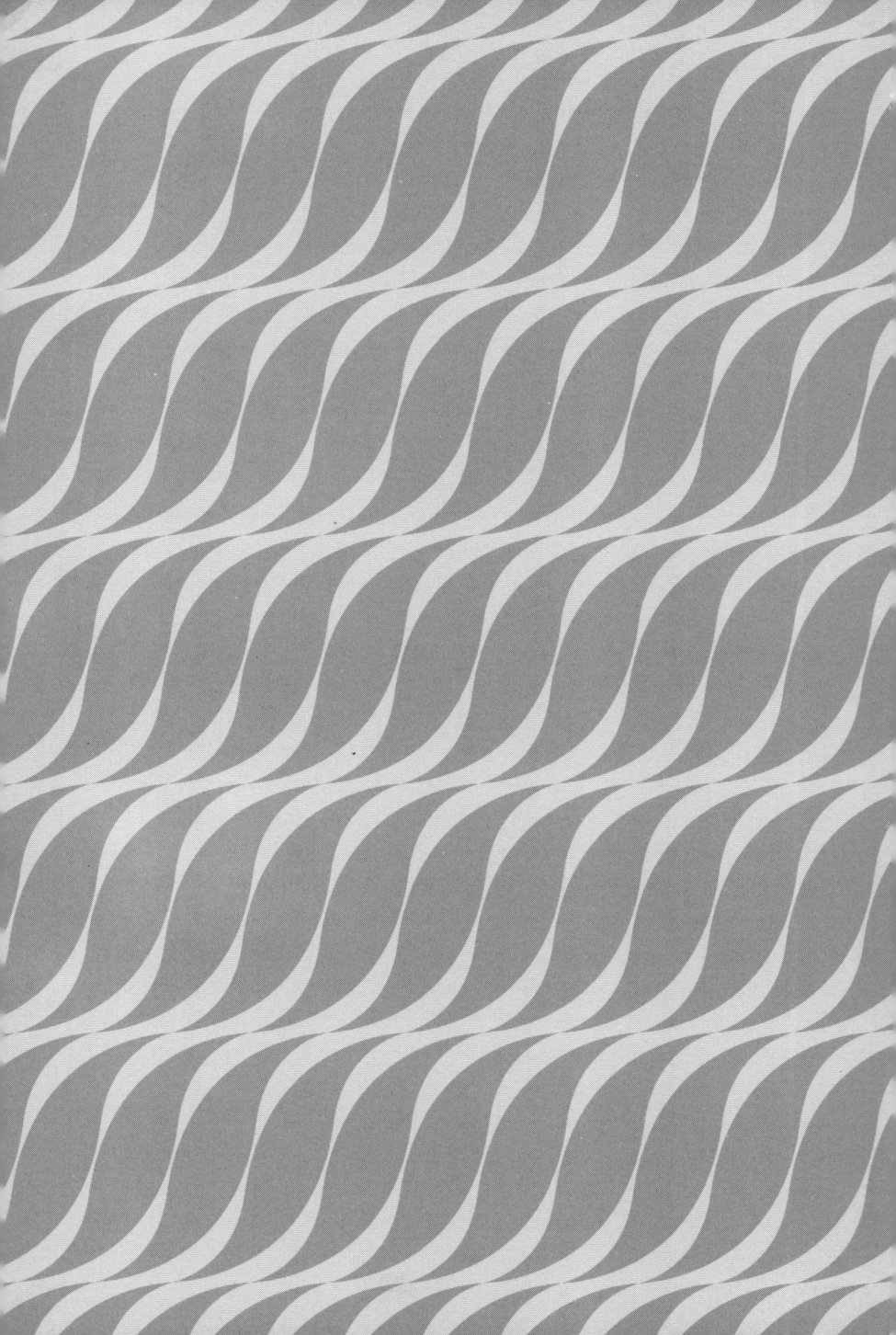